The story of William Booth

Almost every day Mr and Mrs Brown had either a row or a fight. Mr Brown was out of work and felt very bitter about it. Their three eldest children could not get a job either. So there was little or no money coming into the house.

Mrs Brown spent most of her time at the pub. She spent her money there as well. She was often drunk and had nothing left for buying food or clothes.

The family lived in a small damp house in London, near the River Thames. The house was always filthy and the children went around dirty and in rags. For the Brown family there seemed nothing in life to bring them any happiness.

Then one day a friend took Mrs Brown to a Salvation Army meeting. There she heard how God was able to change her life, to make her a new person. When the Salvation Army captain asked if anyone wanted to be "saved", Mrs Brown came forward. She knelt down at a bench, called a "Penitent-form". She prayed to God to forgive her and help her to be a good wife and mother.

From that day on, Mrs Brown was a changed woman. All the family could see that something had happened to her. She stopped drinking, and began to care for her family. She got to work on the house and cleaned it from top to bottom.

What is more, she began to pray. She prayed for her husband to get a job and he got one. She prayed for her three eldest children and they found work as well.

Then she became very ill. She had to go into hospital for an operation. The doctor did not expect her to live. But she was not afraid – her Army friends were praying for her. The operation was a success and she got better.

About a year later, it was decided to pull down the houses in the street where the Brown family lived. The council wanted to know the four best families in the street so they could give them a new house. The Brown family was one of the families chosen.

For over a hundred years now The Salvation Army has been working to "save" people. "Salvation" means "being saved". In the Bible it means being saved by God from all that is wrong and bad in our lives. It includes also being saved from hardships such as poverty, or bad habits like drinking too much alcohol.

The beginning

The Salvation Army was founded in 1865 by William Booth. But that was not its name at first – it used to be called The East London Christian Mission.

William Booth was brought up in Nottingham. When he lost his job he moved to London to find new work. In his spare time he went around preaching, either in churches or on street corners, or anywhere else where people would listen.

After his marriage he was for a few years a Church minister. He preached in churches up and down the country. But this was not what he felt God wanted him to do. He believed God wished him to reach the ordinary people of the land, and therefore he had to take his message to the people in the streets. With his wife Catherine and their children, he returned to London. There were thousands of people in the capital who needed to hear God's word.

One day Booth was asked to preach at an open-air meeting in the East End of London. It was outside the Blind Beggar public house in Whitechapel. A crowd came to listen. They laughed at him and threw bad eggs, but he did not care. When he got home that night he knew what his future was to be.

"I have found my destiny," he told his wife. "I must take the Gospel to the people of the East End."

A few days later he was asked to preach at some meetings in the East End. They were to be held in a large tent on an open space known as Mile End Waste. Booth agreed – this was just the opportunity he wanted.

The meetings in the tent were noisy, with drunks and trouble-makers causing an uproar. Once, the ropes holding up the tent were cut, bringing the tent down on the crowd inside. Another time, winds ripped the canvas, leaving gaping holes that let in the rain.

As the weather became colder, Booth stopped using the tent. For some weeks he rented the East London Theatre. Sometimes he used a dance hall for his meetings, and he even preached in a hayloft.

One of his converts was Peter Monk, a famous Irish boxer. He became Booth's bodyguard. If there was any sign of trouble at a meeting, Monk took off his coat and rolled up his sleeves. While Booth preached, the boxer kept order!

Preaching on the streets

When possible, Booth preached out in the open. His favourite place was outside public houses. In this way he felt he could reach the people who needed his message most. Crowds of people always left the pubs to listen to him. There was usually more fun at these meetings than in the pub! (In those days, of course, there was no radio or television to amuse people.)

As he preached, people jeered and shouted at him, and others were angry at the things he said. Some of the crowd pelted him with bad eggs. He was pushed, and his clothes were torn. Sometimes he was struck by a stone or stick. But he always got up and went on preaching.

The reason why some people were against him was because of the message he preached. "The Bible shows us," he told them, "that we have all sinned against God. God has sent Jesus to die for our sins. We can only be saved if we repent and believe in Jesus."

The idea that God could save people from sin and evil made some people laugh at him.

The work was difficult at first and only a few people accepted his message. At the end of twelve months Booth had sixty people helping him. He called his group "The East London Christian Mission".

Soon he began to open up preaching centres, or "stations" as he called them, in other parts of the East End. A number of rich people who heard about his work, and liked what he was doing, gave him money. In this way, Booth was able to buy a large building in Aldgate. He made it his headquarters and renamed it the People's Mission Hall.

Catherine Booth, William's wife, was now also becoming well known as a preacher. She started some meetings in South London and opened centres at Croydon and Bromley. For the first time, the Mission moved out of East London. As a result, the name of the group was changed. The words "East London" were dropped and it became "The Christian Mission".

London's poor

William Booth cared about poor people. When he saw how they were forced to live, he wanted to do something for them. It was not enough just to preach to them.

As a boy in Nottingham, he had lived among poor people. He

worked in second-hand shops and saw many of them forced to sell even their clothes and shoes for a few pence. As a teenager he searched the streets for them, then led them into church to hear the "good news". Once he found a poor, homeless woman. He and his friends rented a room for her, paying for it out of their own money.

In order to be near the people he wanted to help, he moved house. He took his family to live in the East End. About half a million people lived in that part of London, and most of them were very poor. Now they were his neighbours.

At that time, many families had to live on a very low wage. This meant that they could not afford to pay for somewhere decent to live. A whole family often had to live in only one room. For many of them, there was no bed to sleep on; they had to make do with a few rags on the floor. They were usually too poor to be able to buy food *and* clothing. If they wanted food, then they often had to go without shoes or a coat.

But the worst enemy that Booth had to fight against was drink. Alcohol was cheap, and some people spent all their wages on beer or gin. There were said to be about 100 000 public houses in London. They were open every day of the week, and did not close until midnight. As there were few places where people could go for a night out, the pubs were crowded. For many grown-ups, teenagers and children alike, drinking was their only pastime.

To add to the problem, every fifth shop in the East End was a gin-shop. These shops sold gin even to children, and some had special steps so that little ones could reach up to the counter. Booth often saw five-year-olds drunk, and mothers feeding their babies on beer.

With the aid of his eldest son, Bramwell, now aged sixteen, Booth set to work. He opened a "soup kitchen", where it was possible to buy a hot drink at any time of the day or night. Next he set up five food shops, selling a three-course meal very cheaply.

Children queuing up for a Salvation Army breakfast

To do this, Bramwell used to get up at three o'clock in the morning to push a barrow 4 miles to Covent Garden. He collected vegetables that had been thrown away and bought a few sacks of bones to make a good stew.

Christmas Day at the Booth home was always a happy time. But one Christmas morning, after preaching in Whitechapel, Booth returned home feeling very sad. Walking home through the East End streets, he had seen how some people were keeping the birthday of Jesus – by getting drunk. He was unable to join in with his children's fun and games that day, for thinking about what he had seen.

"I'll never spend another Christmas Day like this again," he told his family. "The poor have nothing but the public house."

Next Christmas it was different. Mrs Booth and some Mission helpers cooked 300 Christmas dinners. The dinners were taken to poor families by Bramwell Booth and other Mission helpers. From that time on, the Booths never spent another Christmas together as a family. They spent the day caring for others in more need than themselves.

The Salvation Army

In the early days of the Mission, many of Booth's helpers began to use army words to talk about their work. It seemed like a war to them, and they were "fighting for God". Helpers were known as "soldiers". When Booth held a big meeting every year to talk to his helpers about their work, he called it a "war congress". And at one time Booth was said to be the "General of the hallelujah army".

Early one morning in May 1878, Booth had a meeting with two of his top leaders. They were talking about Booth's report on the work of the Mission. The report stated at the top of the first page, in capital letters, "THE CHRISTIAN MISSION IS A VOLUNTEER ARMY". (At that time Britain had a volunteer army of part-time soldiers. Everybody made fun of them.)

"Volunteer!" grunted one of the leaders. "I don't belong to the volunteer army. I'm a full-time soldier or nothing."

Booth stopped for a moment, his eyes fixed on the report. He took up a pen and crossed out the word "volunteer". Instead he wrote the word "Salvation".

"Thank God for that," both the leaders said at once.

Before long, the title "Christian Mission" was dropped. Now it was The Salvation Army, and William Booth was its General. It was an Army ready to do battle and to save people.

Marching under the flag

All armies have a flag, and Booth had used one for some years. But in 1878 William Booth's wife Catherine made a new flag for

8

The Salvation Army's flag and crest

the Army station at Coventry. It had a crimson background with blue edging and a sun in the centre.

Four years later the sun was replaced by a star carrying the words "Blood and Fire". The words were to remind the soldiers of the death of Jesus and the baptism of the Holy Spirit. The design has stayed the same ever since.

One of the Army's first officers wrote this about the flag: "The use of the flag has done more than anyone could imagine to bind our soldiers together." In those early days, having a flag gave the Army's soldiers a lot of courage as they marched through the streets.

No army would be complete without a uniform. Almost since

the first days, some of Booth's helpers had begun to wear special dress for their meetings. It was a way of showing people something about their new faith. Many of the men wore dark blue jerseys, carrying either the title "Salvation Army" or perhaps some words from the Bible.

Some of the officers made their own headgear, including army-style caps with home-made badges on them. Henry Howard, a converted builder, went to a meeting with Booth wearing a bowler-hat. Someone gave him a tin label on which the title "Salvation Army" had been punched. He fastened the label to the front of his hat. Others cut out the title of the Army's newspaper, *The War Cry*, and fastened that to their hats.

For a while the women were against the idea of a uniform. And the first officer to wear the Army bonnet almost refused.

Bramwell Booth one day called to see a woman officer. He was holding a bonnet made by the General's wife.

"What do you think of this?" he asked the officer.

"I think it's daft, and I hope you won't expect me to wear it," she replied.

"Yes, I do," Bramwell said. "At tonight's meeting."

"Me? Never!"

But she did, and the bonnet has remained part of the uniform ever since. With just a few small changes, it has stayed the same shape.

The band

Soon after the Army received its new title, the idea of having a band was born. It happened almost by chance.

Army preachers arrived at the city of Salisbury, in Wiltshire, in 1878. Many people in the city did not take to the hearty singing and preaching. Hooligans tried to break up the crowds taking part in the market square services. One man drove a horse and cart straight at the people joining in one meeting.

10

Charles Fry and his three sons turned up at an Army meeting to act as bodyguards. They were all builders by trade, but also played brass instruments. On this day they brought their instruments along with them to help the singing. They were a success. The hooligans stopped their tricks and stayed to listen to the music.

The Fry family – the first Army band

When Booth heard about the event, he wrote to the Frys and asked them to join him on his preaching tours. Anything that would attract a crowd appealed to the General. The Frys sold their building business and went along with Booth as full-time bandsmen.

Up to this time, music in churches and chapels had been provided by either an organ or a piano. The idea of a band horrified some church-goers. But Booth was pleased with the way in which this unusual kind of music helped the preaching. Because there were no radios or record-players, "live" music was a treat for most people.

The General suggested to the Army that they should make more use of all kinds of musical instruments. But as the sound of brass instruments carried better in the open air, they became more popular. Soon Army bands were being set up all over the country.

Some band members began to make up their own music. Others took popular songs of the day and put new words to them. These songs were then sung at Army meetings. For a while the General did not like this idea. But when he realised that ordinary people enjoyed the new songs, then he agreed. "After all," he said to Bramwell, "why *should* the Devil have all the best tunes?"

To all the world

The Salvation Army soon became well known in all parts of Britain. As a result of the open-air preaching, more and more people were being converted to Christianity. And most of these new Christians were ordinary working-class people.

Before long, the Army began to spread to other countries of the world. Again, it was almost by chance. Amos Shirley of Coventry went to America in 1878 to look for a job. Later his wife, together with his daughter, an Army Officer, joined him. The family rented a disused factory in Philadelphia and started holding Army meetings. Soon their services were packed out and they had to find a larger building.

Within weeks Booth sent out a team of officers to help with the work. They opened a centre in New York, followed by ten others in different parts of the country.

Four years later General Booth let it be known that the Army was going to "attack" India. The General sent a team of four officers, led by Major Tucker. Tucker had worked in India for thirty years before joining the Army, and could speak three Indian dialects.

In September 1882 the Army landed at Bombay. The chief of police and a squad of policemen were lined up at the docks to meet them. Major Tucker and his team of three officers marched down the gangway.

"When are your other soldiers going to land?" asked the police chief.

"We are the whole Army," explained Tucker.

"I was expecting at least a thousand of you," said the police chief, his face turning red!

The British Governor of Bombay was opposed to the Army. To make matters worse, Tucker and his officers wore Indian dress. The Governor was shocked by this idea. He did all he could to hold up the Army's work. But despite being sent to prison and receiving threats of death, the Army won through.

The Salvation Army also started work about this time in Australia, Europe, Canada and South Africa. Today there are Army centres in over eighty countries throughout the world.

Army under attack

All was not going well for the Army in England. Although the work was growing fast, the Army was also making enemies. There were people who did not like the gospel they preached,

13

and others were offended by the bands and street meetings. Over a period of four years (1880–84) the Army was stoned or attacked in many kinds of ways.

Once, nine members of the Army band in Torquay were locked up in prison for playing in the streets on a Sunday. Captain Annie Bell was jailed at York for singing in the market-place. In Whitechapel, a group of Army women were roped together then pelted with burning coals. At Hastings a grocer offered bad eggs, free, for throwing at the Army. And at Guildford an Army woman died after being knocked down and kicked.

When Booth was leading a parade while touring the Midlands, someone spat on him. One of his soldiers tried to clean it off.

"Don't rub it off, it's a medal," said the General.

Another time Booth was riding through Sheffield on a wagon. The parade was attacked by a gang known as "The Blades". Stones, eggs, clods of earth and even dead cats were thrown at the soldiers. Through it all the General remained standing upright, giving orders to those who were near him. Afterwards he inspected his soldiers, their uniforms covered with blood, egg-yolks and mud.

"Now is the time to get your photographs taken," he said with a grin.

For the most part, these attacks were taken with a smile and a "God bless you". But on one occasion a certain Mrs Burrell of Manchester lost patience.

"Here's a woman who can work miracles," sneered one man.

"I can't work miracles," she said, "but I can cast out devils." With that, she grabbed the man by the collar and threw him down some stairs!

In one year alone, 669 Army soldiers (both men and women) were knocked down or beaten. Fifty-six Army centres were damaged or totally destroyed. And the police seemed unable to do anything to stop the trouble.

"Skeletons" attacking the Army building at Worthing

Some of the worst troubles came when gangs up and down the country formed what they called a "Skeleton Army". These gangs planned by any means possible to stop the Army's work. They also carried a flag, bearing a picture of either a skeleton or a skull and cross-bones. To show their loyalties, gang members wore a yellow ribbon in their hats.

At Oldham about a hundred young toughs attacked and kicked a group of Army girls. Then at Weston-super-Mare, 2000 "Skeletons" let loose a flock of pigeons in an Army centre. The pigeons had small bags of red pepper tied under their wings. As the birds flew around the hall, the bags dropped and the pepper was scattered over the people in the meeting.

15

In 1884 there was a Skeleton Army of 4000 strong at the south coast town of Worthing. They attacked the Salvation Army soldiers and their building. The police went to the rescue and fought off the Skeletons. But they attacked again and again during the next three weeks. In the end troops were called in and order was restored.

At last the troubles all over the country came to an end and The Salvation Army was allowed to carry on its work. It had won the right to parade peacefully through the streets of England.

Down-and-outs

It was nearly midnight on a cold day one December. The General had been to a meeting in Kent. He caught a cab from London Bridge railway station to his home in the East End.

As his cab crossed the River Thames, he was shocked to see men lying at the side of the road on London Bridge. They were trying to sleep. Some of them were covered with newspapers in order to keep themselves warm.

Next morning his son Bramwell, now grown up, called to see him. Booth was feeling unhappy, still thinking about the homeless men.

"Did you know that men sleep out all night on the bridges?" he asked his son.

"Yes, I have heard about it," replied Bramwell.

"You knew that and you haven't done anything about it?" said the General.

"We can't look after everybody."

"Well, go and do something," Booth told him. "Get hold of a warehouse and warm it. Find the men some clothing and blankets. But mind you, Bramwell, no coddling."

A few weeks later Bramwell found just the place he needed. It was a warehouse in Limehouse, by the West India Docks. It became the Army's first sleeping shelter for down-and-outs.

16

William and Bramwell Booth

A night at the shelter cost fourpence. For this sum a man could also have a towel, soap and hot water for a wash. There was a large bedroom where each man had a mattress to sleep on and a quilt to cover himself. In winter the bedroom was heated.

17

Soon it became the custom for the police to send any man they found wandering the streets to a Salvation Army hostel. Before long the Army had five such shelters for the homeless. Over a thousand men were housed each night. There were Homes for women as well.

Alongside the shelter in Limehouse, Booth opened another food shop. Here food was sold at really cheap prices.

Today the Army in Britain has forty-three hostels for men, and thirteen for women and girls. In addition there are Homes for mothers with children, for mothers expecting babies and for old people.

In Darkest England

There were said to be 3 million people in Britain in the late nineteenth century who did not have enough money to live on. Many of these people were starving or homeless – or both. But nobody seemed to care about them.

The only help given by the Government was in the work-house. The workhouse provided a bed and food in return for a hard day's work. Life here could be cruel and workers were sometimes punished harshly. Most people would rather take to the streets than suffer in that place.

Booth decided that all Britain should know how the poor lived. Together with a friend, he brought out a book called *In Darkest England and the Way Out*. In the book he told of his plans to help the poor and needy. If the Government did not do anything, then he would. He needed £100 000 to start the work and another £30 000 each year to keep it going.

He began to put his plan into action, even though he did not have enough money. First he set up a sort of job centre to help people find work. Then he bought a farm where some of these men could get work and learn to become real people again.

Because 9000 people went missing each year from London

alone, he opened a missing persons bureau. The idea was to find these people and link them up with their families again. He opened more hostels for men. He planned a poor man's bank which made small loans to workers to buy tools or set up in a trade.

He called his plan to help the poor the "Cab-Horse Charter". (There were no taxis in those days, only cabs pulled by horses.) Booth pointed out, "Every cab-horse in London is given food, shelter and work. People ought to be looked after just as well as cab-horses are cared for."

Booth's book sold 200 000 copies in twelve months. The head of the Roman Catholic Church in England, Cardinal Manning, supported Booth. He said that Jesus and his disciples would have done just the same. The famous Baptist preacher, Charles Spurgeon, praised the Army and the work it did.

In the nine years after this book came out, The Salvation Army served 27 million cheap meals, gave lodgings to 11 million homeless people, traced 18 000 missing persons and found jobs for 9000 people out of work.

But the General also had his enemies. One religious organisation stated that poor people ought to help themselves or they would become lazy. Others said that it was not possible to make a worker out of an idle man. Booth did not agree – he had seen too many lives changed by God.

However, Booth's ideas began to spread. Similar plans were started in Europe and as far away as Australia. In America, the Army's work among the poor people made Booth a hero the next time he visited New York. And in India, the British Governor invited the Army to start its work among the worst criminal group in the country.

Death of Catherine Booth

It was about this time that the General suffered a terrible

blow. For two years his wife Catherine had been ill. The doctors could not find a cure for her. Every day she was in pain, yet she still carried on preaching and helping her husband with his work.

At last she had to admit she could do no more. She took to her bed where she was looked after by two nurses, who stayed with her day and night. But there was no hope. With William at her bedside, their sons and daughters came to say "Goodbye". Each one of them came and kissed her. Then with her husband's arms around her, she died – "promoted to glory", as they say in the Army.

When his wife was buried, Booth made a promise – that he would go on spending all his days and hours in serving Christ. Although now sixty years of age, he had his full health and strength. There was still much work to be done, and there were battles to be won.

He next turned his mind to helping the matchmakers of East London. Matches at that time were dipped in a dangerous yellow phosphorus. As the workers often failed to wash their hands before they ate their food, they swallowed some of the poison. Many of them developed a disease known as "phossy jaw". The poison affected the worker's jaw, turning the face green and then black. Soon the victim died.

Wages in these factories were poor, and factory owners did nothing to help those who were ill. One mother and her two children, both aged under nine, worked sixteen hours a day in the match factory. At the end of the week their total pay for making over 1000 boxes was one shilling and threepence, which was worth less than fifty pence in today's money. To fight against this evil, Booth opened his own factory in the East End. It was a clean and well-lit building. Instead of the dangerous yellow phosphorus matches, the factory made safety matches which caused no illness. The workers were paid almost double the wages of those in other factories.

The Army matchboxes carried a special name. They were

called "Lights in Darkest England", after the title of the General's book. At one point, the factory was making 6 million boxes a year.

Ten years later Booth closed down his factory. It was no longer needed. Other matchmaking firms had been forced to follow his idea and produce safety matches. He had won another victory.

Fame

After his wife's death, Booth felt freer to travel and see the Army at work in other countries. The Army by now had centres in twenty-six countries, and the General set out to visit some of them. He made a tour of Europe, paid two visits to America, went to the Holy Land and sailed across the world to Australia.

As early as 1904 the General began to use the newly-invented motor car for his travels around England. In three years he covered 5600 miles by car and preached at nearly 400 meetings. He was seventy-five years old and still going strong.

By now the General was very famous. People crowded to see him wherever he went. Many important people wanted to meet him. In Norway he went to see King Haakon, and in Sweden he was presented to King Gustav. At home, King Edward VII invited him to Buckingham Palace.

"You are doing a good work – a great work," the King told Booth, as he shook his hand.

Booth made friends with many well-known people of the day. He was a friend of Winston Churchill, the man who later became Britain's Prime Minister. Lord Northcliffe, who founded the *Daily Mail*, said he owed all his religion to the General.

As Booth grew older, his eyesight began to fail. One Christmas the General had to admit that he could not see so well. He was taken to Guy's Hospital in London for an operation. But he never fully recovered his sight. His right eye had to be removed and the sight of his other eye became worse.

21

At a meeting at the Albert Hall, he spoke to 7000 Army soldiers. "I am going into dock now for some repairs," he told them. "But while women weep... while little children go hungry ... while men go to prison ... I'll fight to the very end!"

Soon the General was completely blind and his life was drawing to a close. As he was dying he said to his son Bramwell, "I want you to do more for the homeless of the world – if you don't I shall come back and haunt you!"

When the General died he was aged eighty-four years. A notice was put in the Army Headquarters window. It said, "The General has laid down his sword".

William Booth's funeral procession

For three days the General's body rested in an Army Hall in East London. The funeral service was held at Olympia, West London, where 40 000 people came to pay their last respects. Among them, without anyone knowing, was Queen Mary. She sat in a seat at the back of the Hall. Next to her, by the gangway, sat a poorly dressed woman. The woman dropped three faded flowers on the General's coffin as it passed down the gangway.

"Why did you come to the service?" the Queen asked the woman.

"Well," the woman said simply, "he cared for the likes of us."

BIOGRAPHICAL NOTES

William Booth was born in Nottingham in April 1829. He was converted to Christianity at the age of fifteen while attending a Methodist chapel. When he lost his job in a pawnbroker's shop, he moved to London to find work. There he met Catherine Mumford, and they were married in Brixton three years later, in June 1855.

A shoemaker called Edward Rabbits offered to support Booth and his family for at least three months, so that he could give his time to preaching. In 1856 Booth became a minister of the Methodist New Connexion and served as a travelling preacher for nine years. During this time, Catherine also became well known as a preacher.

But Booth was not free to preach where he wanted. He felt called by God to work among the poor people of the East End of London. He gave up his position as a Methodist minister and in 1865 founded The East London Christian Mission. It was not until thirteen years later that the title "Salvation Army" was first introduced (1878).

Soon the Army began to spread – to America (1878), Australia (1880), into Europe (1881), India (1882), South Africa (1891) and Japan (1893).

Other important events include: new Headquarters opened in Queen Victoria Street, London (1881); the first Self-Denial week (1886); Booth's book, *In Darkest England*, published (1890); and the first help ever given by the Army in a disaster, in San Francisco (1906).

Catherine Booth died in 1890, at the age of sixty-one. The General soldiered on for twenty-two more years, and died in August 1912. When he died, he left instructions that his son Bramwell should become the Army's next general.

THINGS TO DO

A Test yourself

Here are some short questions. See if you can remember the answers from what you have read. Then write them down in a few words.

1 When was The Salvation Army first founded?
2 Where did William Booth preach his first sermon in the East End?
3 What did Peter Monk the boxer do to help Booth?
4 For what did Catherine Booth, William's wife, become well known?
5 Who helped Booth set up a "soup kitchen"?
6 Which was the first overseas country to have a Salvation Army centre?
7 Where did General Booth see homeless men sleeping out?
8 Give the title of the book brought out by Booth.
9 What was the promise made by Booth when his wife was buried?
10 What did King Edward VII say to General Booth when he met him at Buckingham Palace?

B Think through

These questions need longer answers. Think about them, then try to write two or three sentences in answer to each one. You may look up the story again to help you.

1 What does the word "salvation" mean? Why did Booth call his Mission "The Salvation Army"?
2 Why did many poor people in Booth's time spend most of their money on drink?
3 What were living conditions like for poor people in the East End of London?
4 Describe some of the attacks made upon The Salvation Army during the years 1880–84.
5 Jesus told his followers: "Go to all peoples everywhere, and make them my disciples." How did General Booth and The Salvation Army carry out this command.

C To talk about

Here are some questions for you to talk about with each other. Try to give reasons for what you say or think. Try to find out all the different opinions which people have about each question.

1 Do you think the title "The Salvation Army" is a good one? Why?

2 Why do you think drinking alcohol is still a wide-spread habit? Does drink make people happy? What sort of problems are caused if people drink too much?

3 Do you think Salvation Army street meetings do any good? Do people prefer to watch religious services on television? Have Christians an important message for people today?

4 What do you think about the Army's social work today among people such as down-and-outs? Is it simply a question of money, or do these people need other kinds of help? Has the Welfare State made the Army's social work unnecessary?

D Find out

Choose one or two of the subjects below and find out all you can about them. History books, geography books and encyclopaedias may be useful. Perhaps you can use reference books in your library to look up some of the names and places.

1 *More about The Salvation Army*
Find out about the work of The Salvation Army today. Here are some ideas to start with:
(a) The Investigation Department – tracing people who have gone missing from home.
(b) Caring for prisoners – visiting them in prison and helping them when they come out.
(c) Feeding the hungry – Major Gardiner's work in Calcutta.
(d) Disaster work – helping in times of great emergency.

2 *Army on the march*
(a) Find out about the various ways in which The Salvation Army is like an ordinary army: the uniform, the flag, the badge and the Army bands.
(b) Visit a local Army centre and find out all about it.
(c) How are the Army's officers trained? What work do they do?

3 *Poor people*
(a) Find out more about how poor people lived in the time of General Booth.
(b) Read about such people as Dr Barnardo, Octavia Hill and Lord Shaftesbury, and write about their work in helping the poor.
(c) What does the organisation called Shelter do for homeless people today?

4 *Down-and-outs*
   (a) How does The Salvation Army care for down-and-outs today?
   (b) Find out about the London Embankment Mission and The Simon Community.
   (c) What help is given to down-and-outs by your local council?
   (d) What makes men and women leave home to wander the streets in this way?

USEFUL INFORMATION

Addresses

Salvation Army Information Services
101 Queen Victoria Street
London EC4P 4EP.

Shelter
157 Waterloo Road
London SE1 8UU.

London Embankment Mission
Webber Street
London SE1 HQA.

The Simon Community
129 Malden Road
London NW5 4NF.

N.B. It is best if only one person in each class writes off for information. Remember to enclose a stamped, addressed envelope for the reply. A postal order for 50p would also be helpful, if you want plenty of material.

More books to read

Army without Guns, by Cyril Barnes (Salvation Army Publishing & Supplies) (P).

Devil's Island, by Brian Peachment (R.E.P.), tells the story of a Salvation Army officer's work among convicts (P).

General Next to God, by Richard Collier (Fontana) (T).

God's Army, by Cyril Barnes (Lion Publishing) (P/T).

A Home for All Children, by Geoffrey Hanks (R.E.P.), tells the story of Dr Barnardo (P).

I Know It Was the Place's Fault, by Des Wilson (Oliphants) (T).

The Salvation Army, by Clifford W. Kew (R.E.P.) (P).

The Welfare State, by R. Cootes, Making the Modern World Series (Longman) (P).

William and Catherine Booth, God's Soldiers, by Jenty Fairbank (Salvation Army Publishing & Supplies) (P).

(T) = suitable for teachers and older pupils
(P) = suitable for younger pupils

Films

What Can Be Done? (33 min), colour. Available from Shelter or Concord Films Council, 201 Felixstowe Road, Ipswich, Suffolk IP3 9BJ.

William Booth – God's Soldier (36 min), black and white. This and other titles available from CTVC Film Library, Foundation House, Walton Road, Bushey, Watford WD2 2JS.

Filmstrips

Victorian Social Life: The Life of the Poor, colour. Available from Longman Group, Pinnacles, Harlow, Essex CM19 5YA.

William Booth (V75) Available from Church Army Filmstrips, 5 Cosway Street, London NW1 5NR.

Slides

Life in Victorian England: Town Life, The Poor (S478), colour, tape or cassette commentary. Available from The Slide Centre, 143 Chatham Road, London SW11 6SR.

Where Do People Live? Available from Shelter.

Pack

Social Problems: Secondary History Pack (Longman).